Euphorbias

Don Wit
(revised edi

Front cover: *Euphorbia characias* – showing different coloured nectaries on the same plant
Photographs by Don Witton
Line drawings by Elaine Walker (pp 37, 43, 50, 52 & 57) and Cyril Stocks (pp 9 & 32)
Editor: Timothy Riggs
©The Hardy Plant Society – October 2010
ISBN 978-0-901687-27-2
First edition: July 2000

View of author's National Collection of euphorbias, in May

The Author

Don Witton is a self-taught horticulturist and plantsman with a passion for perennials in general and euphorbias in particular. He has grown euphorbias for over 20 years and has held a National Collection of hardy forms since 1998. Having now retired from school teaching he runs a small nursery specialising in euphorbias, and lectures to groups all over the country. (See website for details.) Don would like to thank his long-suffering wife, Dot, for her patience, understanding and tolerance of his passion over many years. She has acquired her own comprehensive knowledge of the genus from being exposed to it for such a long period.

The Illustrators

Elaine Walker is a passionate plantswoman who opens her garden regularly to the public. She is an active member of a number of garden clubs, including the Nottingham Group of the HPS.

Cyril Stocks took up botanic art as a retirement activity and reached a very high standard, meeting the Queen as a result of his work. He was a life-long gardener and member of the Dorset Group of the HPS. Cyril died during the production of this booklet.

2

INTRODUCTION

The family *Euphorbiaceae* is the sixth-largest family of flowering plants. The genus *Euphorbia* makes up by far the greatest proportion of the family, and with over 2000 species it is the largest plant genus in the world. *Euphorbia* species can be found growing on every continent except Antarctica, exhibiting a huge range and variety of forms and plant types, from annuals and biennials to leafy perennials, woody shrubs and trees. Depending on their climatic origin, most euphorbias can be found in both hardy and tender forms. For example, *E. mellifera*, from the Canary Islands, is an evergreen shrub, hardy to around −12°C, while *E. pulcherrima* (better known as poinsettia, which is sold by the thousands as a house plant during the Christmas period), is a tender, 2m deciduous shrub from Central America. But the vast majority of euphorbias are succulents, and come mostly from the continent of Africa. Indeed the tree-like succulent, *E. candelabrum*, found in southern African countries, grows into one of the strangest looking plants on the planet.

E. candelabrum (Southern Africa) Las Palmas Botanic Garden, Gran Canaria

Of the 2000 or more species of *Euphorbia*, only around 200 will cope with our British climate and can therefore be used as garden plants. These leafy perennials come mainly from Europe and temperate Asia. Europe has around 100 native species, and about a dozen of these grow wild in the UK.

This book focuses mainly on those leafy, hardy perennials and shrubs which can be grown outside in British gardens. Within this group there are varieties suitable for every garden situation, and many gardeners view them as an essential component of their garden borders.

Some myths have sprung up about euphorbias. For instance, they are regularly stated as having green flowers. While it is true that the variety of foliage and form is far wider than the colour of the flowers, the floral colour starts from shades of lime, through lemon, yellow, gold, buff and into orange and reds. There are even one or two rarer white forms. Plants grown in a lot of shade will not display their boldest colour and will tend to have more green pigments, as the colour comes from modified floral leaves, or bracts (see Botany). More exposure to sun will give richer colours, and these persist over a longer period than in most plants with petaloid flowers. Indeed, the flowering period for many euphorbias may extend from late January to beyond November, the peak month being May.

Another myth is that euphorbias are invasive, and can take over the garden. Again, while the great diversity of species includes those that produce copious amounts of viable seed, or spread by underground runners, there are also forms that will remain in a neat clump without seeding or running. If you do not like seeding and running plants in your garden, stick to the well-behaved clumpers (see the A–Z Section for details.) Seeding species, such as *EE. lathyris*, *stricta* and *hyberna*, are annuals, biennials or short-lived perennials, and as with any plants with a short life span, they will produce copious amounts of seed to continue the species. For these species, dead-head to avoid unwanted seed dispersal and hoe out any stray seedlings in the spring. Species that spread by runners, for example *EE. cyparissias* and *robbiae*, will need thinning out every 2–3 years depending on where they are sited. The roots of running species are not deep and are relatively easy to dig out.

Another complaint is that euphorbias are big, and outgrow their space. The wide range of forms in the genus does indeed include species such as *E. wulfenii*, which can reach 1.5m, and *E. nereidum* and the hybrid shrub *E. x pasteurii*, which can be well over 2m, but one of the fascinations of garden euphorbias is that they offer such a range of heights, from *E. capitulata* (5cm) to the 2m giants. There are plenty of forms of around 50–60cm which are eminently suitable for the smaller border. The larger forms can always be cut back to maintain their shape.

Some garden euphorbias were thought to be of questionable hardiness, as many come from the Atlantic Islands and the Mediterranean region, but with the effects of global warming in the last decade this no longer applies, provided the plants are not grown in waterlogged or exposed positions.

So, despite some perceived drawbacks, the genus *Euphorbia* has plenty of good garden-worthy plants suitable for a wide range of locations. This is confirmed by the Royal Horticultural Society, which has given 17 varieties an Award of Garden Merit (AGM). It is a fact that euphorbias give a zingy vibrancy to garden borders, especially in springtime.

BACKGROUND INFORMATION

HISTORY

Euphorbias have been observed and recorded since Ancient Greek times, but the three common herbaceous species, 'Paralios', 'Myrtites' and 'Characias', described by Greek writers were given the generic name 'Tithymalus', and the succulent forms were thought to be unrelated. According to Roger Turner, the name 'euphorbia' was probably first used in Roman times, when it is said that King Juba II of Mauretania (52BC–23AD) discovered a plant (probably the succulent *E. resenifera* from Morocco) and named it after his physician, Euphorbus.

Subsequent herbaceous euphorbias were all classified under the Tithymalus name and the succulent euphorbias continued to be regarded as a separate genus. The first person to make a botanical link between *Euphorbia* and *Tithymalus* was Andrea Cesalpino, an Italian physician, philosopher and botanist, in 1583, but it wasn't until 1753 that Linnaeus placed both groups of plants in the genus *Euphorbia*, which now contains 2160 known species.

The English common name of 'spurge' derives from the Old French 'espurgier' which originated from the Latin word 'expurgare' (meaning to purge out), due to the use of the plant's sap as a purgative.

GEOGRAPHICAL DISTRIBUTION

As already stated, different species can be found growing in every corner of the planet except Antarctica. Being so widespread, euphorbias have evolved many forms and strategies to cope and survive in the habitats and climatic conditions they experience. As well as the herbaceous perennials, which inhabit temperate climates, and succulent forms which hail from tropical arid zones, there are annuals (the petty spurge, *E. peplus*, is a common but not pernicious garden weed), biennials (*E. lathyris*, a species which resembles no other), shrubs and trees. A few examples of their worldwide distribution are:-

Succulents

India –	*E. neriifolia*
S Africa –	*E. horrida*
	E. mauretanica
Kenya –	*E. candelabra*
Madagascar –	*E. milii*
Morocco –	*E. resinifera*
Brazil –	*E. sipolsii*
Canary Islands –	*E. canariensis*
	E. aphylla

Shrubs

Mexico –	*E. pulcherrima*
	E. fulgens
Azores –	*E. stygiana*
Mediterranean Islands –	*E. spinosa*
	E. dendroides

Herbaceous Perennials

New Zealand –	*E. glauca*
Australia –	*E. terracina*
Eastern Asia –	*E. pekinensis*
Nepal –	*E. griffithii* *E. schillingii*
Western Asia –	*E. soongarica* *E. sarawschanica*
Southern Europe –	*E. polychroma* *E. characias* *E. rigida*
England –	*E. amygdaloides* *E. portlandica*
Morocco –	*E. nereidum*
North America –	*E. marginata* *E. corollata*

The hardy herbaceous and woody species come mainly from Europe, especially southern Europe (Crete alone has over 30 species), and temperate Asia. They grow in a relatively narrow band stretching from China in the east (*E. pekinensis*) to the Azores in the west (*E. stygiana*). The northern limit is southern Scandinavia (*E. palustris*), and the southern limit is the Atlas mountains in Morocco (*E. nereidum*). From the gardener's point of view there are three notable species which do not come from this band. These are *E. glauca* (New Zealand) and *E. marginata* and *E. corollata* (North America). All these species benefit from winter protection and can be regarded as half hardy.

Euphorbias can be found growing in mountains, woodland, open country and at or near to the coast. Indeed the sea spurge, *E. paralias*, inhabits sandy shorelines from England to the Middle East. Growing at the highest altitude is *E. wallichii*, which can survive at 4000m on the border between Nepal and Tibet.

BOTANY

Apart from the sap, the one unifying feature of all euphorbias is their unique floral structure. The make-up of the flower is quite complex, consisting of a small cup-shaped organ called a *cyathium* (plural *cyathia*) occurring singly, in pairs, or groups of three. Growing from the top of each cyathium is a female flower with 3 fused ovaries, each containing one ovule. The male flowers are grouped around this female flower and reach maturity later, thus reducing self-pollination. On the outside lip of the cyathium are glands, or *nectaries*, that secrete nectar to attract and reward insect pollinators, commonly flies, bees, wasps and ants. The nectaries can be horseshoe-, crescent- or kidney-shaped, depending on species, and their colour can range from almost black to brown, buff, yellow, orange and red. In some species, most notably *E. mellifera*, the nectaries exude a rich, sweet perfume. A number of varieties have been named after the nectary colour, for example 'Black Pearl' and 'Perry's Tangerine'. This can create problems, as nectaries can be a different colour, not only in the same species but also on the same plant. This occurs most commonly in *E. characias*, and has led to a large number of garden seedlings receiving cultivar names, though differing little from the species (see under *E. characias*).

After pollination, the ovary swells and ripens into a three-sectioned fruit capsule, each section containing one seed. These seed capsules are roughly spherical in shape but can vary considerably from species to species. They remain on the plant, drying and shrinking until they burst open with an audible crack and propel their seeds in all directions. All euphorbias disperse their seeds in this way and as some species flower as early as February–March, these explosions can be heard in the garden from June onwards.

Most euphorbia seeds are ovoid in shape with a hard, smooth shell. They range in colour from dark brown to light brown and grey. Seeds of *E. myrsinites* are unusual in being cylindrical, with a rough-textured surface. All seeds have a small visible growth at one end known as a *caruncle*. This contains an oil-rich substance said to attract ants, which carry off the seed and thus disperse it even further. The seeds are relatively large, ranging in length from 1.5mm (*E. portlandica*) to 5mm (*E. lathyris*).

Most of the euphorbias described in this book are multi-stemmed, leafy, herbaceous perennials. Also listed are annuals, biennials and shrubs suitable for outdoor cultivation.

Of the herbaceous varieties, the stems can be either annual or biennial. Species with annual stems will die back in the autumn, by which time the plant has already

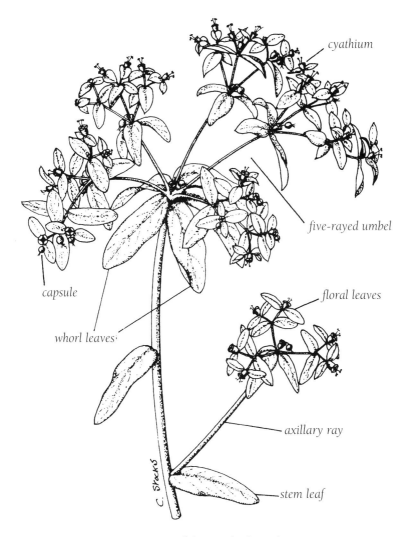

cyathium

five-rayed umbel

capsule

floral leaves

whorl leaves

axillary ray

stem leaf

C. Stocks

Structure of the euphorbia plant

produced new growth buds, usually visible at or just above soil level. From the following January onwards, when the weather is favourable, these buds will start to show signs of new growth. The new stem and leaf growth rarely suffers frost damage when the weather turns cold, so shouldn't need any protection. Species with biennial stems will produce shoots one year, which will then over-winter with foliage on before flowering the following spring. The stems will then die back from late spring through until autumn, depending on species.

Both evergreen and annual forms will start to drop their leaves from the lower half of the stems as they grow and reach full flowering height. This is a natural process in all euphorbias but it doesn't generally detract from their appearance in the garden as they mostly have upright bushy forms. The only examples where bare stems could be an issue are the prostrate species *E. myrsinites* and *E. capitulata*. If plants become stressed, for example from lack of water if grown in a pot, they could defoliate much further up the stem. This is a strategy the plants adopt in the wild to help them survive drought conditions.

Euphorbias have three distinct types of leaf: stem, whorl and floral.

Stem leaves
In the euphorbias listed in this book, the stem leaves range from linear to oblong. They do not have stalks (petioles) and their edges are smooth or very occasionally slightly serrated. Leaf arrangement on the stem is usually alternate, but can occasionally be spiral. *E. lathyris* is the only species in which the leaves are arranged

E. sikkimensis (emerging foliage) – February

10

in opposite pairs, with each pair being at right angles to the pairs immediately above and below. Leaf colour varies from deep glossy green or pale soft-textured green, to blue-grey or purple, with a number of forms having variegated foliage with yellow, cream or off-white edges. Some of the Himalayan species and hybrids have a pretty maroon perimeter to the leaf and *E. sikkimensis* exhibits bright pink colours. Leaf length can vary enormously, from diminutive, in *E. capitulata* (<1cm) to the tropical-looking leaves of *E.* x *pasteurii*, which can reach 30cm.

Whorl leaves
At the top of the main stem in many species there is a distinct collar or whorl of leaves. The whorl leaves are often a different shape from the stem leaves. Above this collar there is an umbel-like branching flower head which often starts with five branches and then divides up to twice more.

Floral leaves
At the end of the dividing stems are the flowers, which are unique in having neither petals nor sepals. The floral, or cyathium leaf, provides the colour, as already described.

The roots of most euphorbias are thick, fleshy and branching. Large clump-forming Asian species like *E. palustris* develop a large, solid, corky mass before the roots start branching, and with *E. griffithii* and its forms, the fleshy roots travel considerable distances horizontally before shooting. The roots of some of the Mediterranean species are more woody, and *E. characias* and its subspecies have a tap root. Some species, most notably *E. cyparissias* and *E. amygdaloides* var. *robbiae*, have much more fibrous roots and will creep and spread by underground runners. To some gardeners this is an undesirable fault. (If you wish to avoid these forms consult the A–Z list for warnings!)

EUPHORBIAS IN THE GARDEN

Euphorbias hardy enough to be grown outside in our British gardens are a versatile group, and there are varieties to enhance most garden situations. The glaucous-leaved species, for example, *EE. nicaeensis, myrsinites* and *rigida*, like hot, sunny, well-drained positions such as rock gardens, scree beds and containers, whilst *E. palustris* revels in damp, wet conditions and is ideal for pond or streamside planting. *E. griffithii* and its cultivars thrive on heavier clay soils and remain relatively compact, whilst *E. amygdaloides*, the wood spurge, prefers a humus-rich soil and dappled shade. *E. amygdaloides* var. *robbiae* will grow in a sunny aspect but is best known because it will survive, thrive and flower in dry shade. Sizes vary from the miniature *E. capitulata* to the stately *E. characias* subsp. *wulfenii* and even taller summer-flowering *E. soongarica*. And then there are many cultivars, for example *E. polychroma*, which, at around 60cm, make great border perennials. There are also several shrubs, from the low-growing *E. spinosa* to the much taller, bushy, *E. mellifera*.

Another good reason for incorporating euphorbias into planting schemes in the garden is that roughly half of the species and forms are evergreen, providing plenty of colour (greens, blues, purples and variegated) to cheer us up during the coldest and darkest months of the year.

CULTIVATION

Most euphorbias are quite accommodating, and will grow well and tolerate conditions which are not ideal. For example, the swamp spurge, *E. palustris*, will cope without extra moisture, and the Mediterranean spurge, *E. characias*, while happiest in full sun, will tolerate partial shade. As a general rule, however, euphorbias prefer some sun, shelter, and reasonable drainage.

Many gardening books will state that euphorbias need to grow in 'ordinary' garden soil, but what does this mean? In practice it means they will grow in a fair range of soils, and tolerate a wide range of pH values, from limy chalk to humus acid soils. Best is a well-drained friable soil, which can be sandy, gravelly or loamy. Worst is heavy clay soil. To achieve a good friable soil add some well-rotted manure or compost into the planting mix unless you already have a very rich soil. Even glaucous-leaved species, which are normally found in thin, impoverished conditions in the wild, will cope with this treatment.

When replacing an old plant with a new euphorbia the best course is to dig out a fair amount of soil and replace it with fresh soil containing some compost. There is no scientific evidence that euphorbias suffer from soil sickness, like roses, but from experience, soil around the roots can get very compacted over the years and new plants will grow away far better if this advice is taken.

Bare-rooted euphorbias need to be planted in the dormant season (November to early March) but pot-grown plants can be planted at any time of year as long as the soil is not frozen or waterlogged. Once the location is selected and the soil prepared, dig out a good-sized hole and place the plant in the middle with the top of the root ball at soil level. Then infill the hole, firming gently, and complete by lightly raking the soil surface around the base of the plant. Water well, and, if the weather remains dry, continue watering until the plant is putting on new growth. Once established, euphorbias should rarely need watering.

Evergreen forms grown in exposed locations will benefit from some winter protection for their first couple of winters, as one of their main enemies is winter gales. Even when fully established and mature, all forms of *E. characias*, especially the taller varieties, can suffer from wind-rock, and it is not unknown for sections of the plant to be snapped off from the woody base in winter storms. To counter this, some form of staking may prove beneficial in less sheltered positions. Most euphorbias should not need staking, although some of the Asian species, such as *EE. palustris, villosa, sarawschanica* and *soongarica*, can make big plants, especially after flowering, and may need staking to keep them relatively compact. The stakes need to be in place early so that the plants can grow above them and look more natural later in the season.

Another winter hazard for evergreen herbaceous plants is snow cover (shrubs should generally cope with snowy conditions.) The weight of snow may damage plants by bending down and breaking the stems. If snow persists, it should be carefully knocked off as soon as possible to maintain the plant's shape. During severe frosty weather, evergreen foliage will droop down and look sad, but the leaves will make surprisingly quick recoveries once the weather warms up.

PRUNING

Annual stems
For varieties which die back at the end of the growing season, (generally October,

E. characias 'Perry's Winter Blusher' in February

but *E. polychroma* and its forms can maintain some leaves until December) pruning is fairly straightforward. Simply cut back all the dead top-growth as near to ground level as possible. By this time most species have already produced new buds which will be visible at, or just above ground level. The major exceptions to this are the forms of *EE. griffithii* and *dulcis*, which will not produce new above-ground growth until late winter.

Prunings can be composted, but in practice it is easier to let them dry and then burn them, as many old stems may be woody, and will take years to rot down.

Evergreen stems

The evergreen varieties, although perennial, flower on a biennial cycle. This means that they grow stems one year and flower on these in the second year. After flowering and seeding, the stems die and turn brown, dropping all their leaves. At the same time, new stems are being produced lower down, near the base of the plant. Cut out all of the old stems, right down to this new emerging growth (the stems of *E. wulfenii* can be well over 1m long and quite woody towards the bottom).

14

Perform this task when the old flowering stems are no longer contributing any garden worthiness and the colour fades from green to pale yellow and eventually brown and crisp, as they do in the wild. Normally this is from June to mid-August, depending on variety. The height of the plants will be reduced by up to a half. The new, lower stems will grow during the late summer and autumn, contributing a fresh foliage appearance. Gardeners who wish to save seed may leave this task later than others to ensure that the seed capsules fully ripen and as much viable seed as possible can be collected.

A more detailed list of garden tasks and when to perform them can be found at the end of this book.

PESTS AND DISEASES

Euphorbias have very few enemies, and will rarely show any signs of pest damage – probably because of their sap. In many parts of the Mediterranean, whole fields and hillsides can be seen grazed bare of all vegetation by semi-wild goats, but euphorbias stand alone and untouched. They are a popular choice as rabbit- and deer-proof plants. Slugs and snails are also rarely seen on plants. Very occasionally slugs have been known to nip out the softest tip at the end of a shoot. This can be very annoying if it happens to be a tip cutting of a choice variety but it is quite unusual on mature plants.

Some greenfly can be attracted to the growing tips of new stems in spring, as can whitefly to the underside of stem leaves. This can be more of a problem if plants are in a greenhouse for the winter. In the garden, they will hardly be noticeable and will not affect growth.

The only other pest worthy of note is the larva of the tortrix moth. This small (1cm), olive-green caterpillar encloses itself in a rolled up leaf which it glues together with a white sticky substance. This not only looks unsightly but can also disfigure leaves. Once again this is a bigger problem in the greenhouse than it will ever be in the garden. Keep an eye out for any signs from late February onwards and, if spotted, just rub them out.

Disease can be more of a problem, especially powdery mildew, which is worst on the dark maroon- and purple-leaved varieties, especially *EE. amygdaloides* 'Purpurea', *dulcis* 'Chameleon', numerous forms of *E. x martinii*, and 'Nothowlee' (**Blackbird**). Other species may show signs of mildew if they become pot-bound or stressed in any way. The secret is to give these plants the conditions they require and keep them growing as strongly as possible. New growth is not usually affected.

In really wet summers, rust may become a problem, especially in species *EE. characias, cyparissias, dulcis* and their cultivars. Orange spots appear on the leaves – especially the undersides – and stems become defoliated rather more than they would in a normal year. In our current climate and depending on where you live, rust may be a problem roughly every five or six years.

The above pests and diseases can be controlled by spraying, but none is a major problem, and many gardeners will prefer to let nature look after itself. Good garden practice, hygiene, and a diverse ecosystem to encourage wildlife, should minimise any adverse effects.

PLANT ASSOCIATIONS

For maximum impact on the garden scene, euphorbias really need to be grown in association with other plants. Too many euphorbias together in one area would be brash in the spring and boringly monochrome in the summer.

The choice of plant associations is wide, and a matter of personal taste, but there are a few general points worth noting: the colour wheel shows that the best colour to associate with euphorbia yellow is blue, running into deeper shades of purple; for contrast, bright reds look good with euphorbia yellow; pinks usually clash, especially with the fiery reds of *E. griffithii* and its cultivars; summer-flowering euphorbias give the most impact when grown with plants having blue or red flowers at around the same time.

Blue flowers are in short supply in late winter and early spring when the euphorbia flowering season begins. Pulmonarias make cheerful ground-cover in and amongst early-flowering plants, especially those with rich blue flowers like *PP. longifolia*, 'Smoky Blue' and 'Diana Clare'. A little later, brunneras will add frothy blues to the scene. Good varieties include *B. macrophylla* 'Hadspen Cream' and 'Jack Frost'. Adding height and blue flowers in mid-spring, we can use the short-lived *Erysimum* 'Bowles's Mauve', and irises, *II. pallida* and *sibirica*, with a large selection in every shade of blue and purple. Spring-flowering bulbs are also good partners, whether used in the rock garden or border. The low-growing *Muscari* is very pretty, and the later and taller *Camassia leichtlinii* works well with medium-sized euphorbias like *E. polychroma*.

Bulbs also work well when it comes to using red. *E. myrsinites* looks stunning grown through dwarf red tulips. But look no further than any of the red forms of *E. griffithii* to grow alongside any number of yellow euphorbias to make a vibrant colourful spectacle during May. There are no red, summer-flowering euphorbias, but this eye-catching red/acid yellow combination can be created in the summer herbaceous border by using other genera. In July, for instance, *E. cornigera* looks stunning with *Monarda* 'Gardenview Scarlet', as does *E. schillingii* with *Crocosmia* 'Lucifer' in August.

Other individual combinations you may like to try are:

February/March:
Yellow- or maroon-flowering *Helleborus* **x** *hybridus* and **Redwing**

April:
Pulsatilla vulgaris and *E. myrsinites*

May:
Allium 'Globemaster' and *E. fragifera*

Late May/early June:
Campanula glomerata 'Superba' and *E. nicaeensis*

June:
Blue-leaved hostas, especially *H.* 'Halcyon', and *E. donii*

June/July:
Geranium ibericum and *E. cognata*

And finally, try two plants which associate well but flower at different times, *Geranium* 'Ann Folkard' and *E. griffithii* 'Dixter'. 'Ann Folkard' has pale yellowy-green leaves and is a small emerging clump when 'Dixter' is showing off throughout May and early June. By the time 'Ann Folkard' is flowering in June and July, 'Dixter' has finished flowering and provides a structure of multi-stemmed, bloodshot foliage for the long stems of 'Ann Folkard' to rest amongst and display its stunning rich cerise-pink flowers randomly throughout. Extremely effective and pretty.

CUT FLOWERS

Many people are not aware that there are numerous varieties of euphorbias which make very good cut flowers. They are very popular with flower clubs and church groups as they can be used in their floral arrangements. A vase of *E. characias* stems makes a floriferous and unusual display. Euphorbias are eminently suitable for large bold arrangements, as many of the species with long straight stems do have large branching inflorescences. Good examples include *EE. palustris, villosa, soongarica, schillingii, donii, griffithii*, and some of the hybrids, like **Excalibur** and *E.* **x** *martinii*. Perhaps the most popular species used in flower arranging are *EE. oblongata* and *marginata*.

The problem of caustic sap must be kept in mind when using euphorbias in flower arranging. The best way to staunch the flow of sap when the stems are cut is to push them gently into moist soil or place them in a bucket of water for a few minutes. Another practice is to singe the cut ends in a candle flame.

PROPAGATION

Some species propagate themselves with no effort on the part of the gardener, either by seeding around or spreading by underground runners; the hardest problem is restraining them. Others, (most notably *E. characias* cultivars and some glaucous-leaved forms) can prove extremely difficult to propagate. Some cultivars will produce good garden plants from seed, but they may be variable and not come true to type. Indeed this is how many new garden hybrids have arrived and been given cultivar names. Most named cultivars need to be propagated vegetatively i.e. through cuttings or divisions, to keep the genetic make-up exactly the same. However, *EE. amygdaloides* 'Purpurea', *dulcis* 'Chameleon', *marginata* 'Summer Icicle' and *rigida* 'Sardis' can all be propagated from seed and should mostly come true to type. Less strongly coloured seedlings should be rogued out.

SEED

A number of species and their forms (especially *EE. characias, dulcis, myrsinites*, and short-lived species like *EE. hyberna* and *lathyris*) will readily produce seedlings in the garden, especially if grown near gravel, so seed of these species and also of *E. polychroma*, can be sown outside in autumn, and will benefit from a winter chilling. Ideally they should be sown in gritty seed compost and covered with a thin layer of grit. This will keep the surface loose and prevent green algae from developing on the surface of the compost. Emerging seedlings will push through without any problem. Pots should be placed in open trays or cold frames, covered only with small wire mesh to keep mice out. Germination will occur the following spring, and should produce strong seedlings for pricking out and growing on.

Alternatively all seed, including that from less-hardy species, can be sown from February onwards under plastic propagating covers, either in the greenhouse or in pots in a cold frame. Once again, cover compost with about 1cm of sharp grit. If bottom heat is used, germination will be quicker, but once the seedlings have emerged, remove from the heat or they will become leggy. Seeds sown from April onwards don't need covering provided they are kept watered. Once the seedlings have produced at least two true leaves, prick them out into small pots. As the plants grow and develop they can be moved up a pot size (say to 1 litre pots) from where they can eventually be planted out in the garden. Some of the less-hardy or rarer forms can be potted on again in early autumn, overwintered in a cold greenhouse and planted out the following spring. This will ensure a stronger, larger plant that will be able to cope better with life in the open garden.

Collecting seed is quite straightforward. Just cut the old stems when the plump fruits are turning a dull green to brown (they will start to crack and disperse their seed on warm sunny days when ripe). Place them head down in a large paper bag, label it, and store in a dry place until the end of the season. Because different species flower at different times of the year, mature seed is produced at different times. Early-flowering species like *EE. rigida* and *myrsinites* produce their seed from late May onwards, *E. lathyris* will still have lots of seed on the plant in September. Some of the summer- flowering species may not produce viable seed, as the climate may not stay warm for long enough to ripen the seed.

The dried stems can be safely removed from their paper bags from late September. By this time the seed will have split from the dried fruit shells and be at the bottom of the bag. Use a small paintbrush to separate the seed from the debris. Any white seed should be discarded, as it has not ripened. Store the seed in paper envelopes in the refrigerator until required for sowing.

CUTTINGS

Cuttings can be taken at any time during the growing season but the best time is from May to July. From the end of June onwards most spring-flowering types, which are the vast majority, will have finished flowering and produced excellent cutting material at the top of the stems from beneath the faded inflorescences. Cuttings from *E. characias* and its cultivars will be more successful if they are taken sooner rather than later, and the best cutting material is from the thinner stems low down on the plant. It is important that all equipment is clean and sterile to avoid fungal diseases which can rot the cutting material.

When taking cuttings it is a good idea to wear surgical rubber gloves. Using a sharp knife, cut 5–10cm shoots from the tip of healthy new growth and remove the lower leaves. This will produce copious amounts of sap. To staunch the flow, gently press the cut end into the soil. Alternatively drop the cuttings into a container of water. This is a good idea if you are taking a lot of cuttings from one plant. The water will turn milky but the sap will have ceased flowing when they are taken out. After removing the cutting material from the water, leave to drain for a few minutes before continuing. Dip the cut end of the stems in hormone rooting powder or liquid, and dib the lower half of the cutting into a rooting medium. The compost needs to be free-draining but be able to hold moisture. A good medium is 50-50 cutting compost and vermiculite with a little sharp sand added to the mix, but gardeners may have their own recipes and preferences.

Euphorbia cuttings will generally benefit from not being covered, as they dislike humidity. Provided the compost is kept moist and the cuttings are kept in the shade they will not wilt, and fungal rotting will be greatly reduced. However, cuttings from some of the Asian species, which grow naturally in more moist conditions, will benefit from having a plastic propagating cover over them for a couple of weeks to prevent wilting. After that the covers can come off. Species which will benefit from this are *EE. palustris*, *villosa*, *soongarica* and *griffithii*.

New growth from the top of the cuttings will indicate that they have rooted. Cuttings taken early in the year can then be potted up, but those taken in July and August can be left over winter before potting up and growing on. Whichever method is adopted, cuttings can be grown on, potted on again if required and planted out when they have a good root system.

An alternative method for shrubby species like *EE. mellifera*, **x** *pasteurii*, and *characias* and its cultivars, is to take the equivalent of hardwood cuttings. Cut 30cm straight stems in spring or summer, strip the leaves from the lower half, and after making a hole in the soil with a spike or cane, insert it into the ground. Water regularly, especially during dry periods, and leave until the following spring. Once again, new growth will indicate that roots have formed. Carefully dig up and pot up. Expect some stems to rot in the winter, but successful results will be achieved.

DIVISION

Most clump-forming and running species and their hybrid forms can be increased by division. Plants can be dug up and divided, or, in the case of large mature clumps, a large piece of the crown can be dug away from the main plant still in the ground. This is reasonably easy for *EE. griffithii* and *sikhimensis*, digging up long, fleshy, bleached underground stems, but species like *EE. palustris*, *soongarica* and *villosa*, which have thick woody crowns, are hard to penetrate with a spade unless you are strong and determined. If the hole is back-filled with fresh soil the main plant should not be unduly affected. This is a good way of reducing the footprint of mature plants in the garden bed, as they can cover a lot of soil surface. *E. characias* and its cultivars, although looking and growing like clump-forming perennials, have a central tap root, so division is not an option. Also, this method of propagation will not work with glaucous-leaved species like *EE. myrsinites*, *rigida* and *nicaeensis*.

The best time to divide euphorbias is during the dormant season, preferably October and February.

Once you have a full plant or large piece before you, it can be split into any number of divisions, large or small, depending on your needs and requirements. To do this you will need a strong sharp knife. Provided there is at least one growth bud joined to part of a piece of root, it should re-grow successfully. Even small pieces with sections of woody underground growth and no fibrous roots can be encouraged to grow with careful watering, but divisions with some fibrous root attached will grow away more quickly.

Large divisions can be planted straight out in their new positions in the garden, and smaller pieces can be potted up. In either case, replant with the growth buds protruding above soil level, as they would have been originally. Keep well watered and the division will soon start putting on new top growth. Most divisions should flower in their first year, but the plants are unlikely to grow to their full size in this time.

AN A–Z LISTING

In the ten years since the first edition of this booklet was published, the RHS *Plant Finder* has listed about 50 new garden euphorbias. Some are new species from the wild, introduced by botanic gardens or seed companies, for example *E. margalidiana*, whilst others, such as 'Whistleberry Garnet', are good garden hybrids, and will deservedly earn their keep in the garden. But beware – some of the newer forms are no improvement on older, similar, forms, or just poor unstable specimens. Care needs to be taken when selecting which plants to buy.

Most of the euphorbias available to the British gardener are listed here. Many are quite common and will be found at any good garden centre, while others may need a little tracking down. Species are more reliably named in the trade, with the exception of *E. wallichii* (see entry), than cultivars, especially those of *E. characias*. Some named cultivars may differ slightly from the descriptions given, depending on where the plant was sourced.

Some of the species appear under synonyms, particularly the following:

E. biglandulosa	- see *E. rigida*
E. epithymoides	- see *E. polychroma*
E. longifolia	- see *E. donii*
E. reflexa	- see *E. seguieriana* subsp. *niciciana*
E. serrulata	- see *E. stricta*
E. uralensis	- see *E.* x *pseudovirgata*
E. x *waldsteinii*	- see *E. virgata*
E. stricta	- sometimes found as 'Golden Foam', but this name is invalid.

The euphorbias have been placed into three groups for ease of reference and to help with selection of the type of plant required. These are:

1) short-lived plants (including annuals and biennials)
2) shrubs
3) perennials

The last group makes up the majority of the list and includes both herbaceous and evergreen forms.

An indication of plant hardiness is given by a Z rating, which relates to the American system of plant-hardiness zones: Z4 being extremely hardy, surviving temperatures as low as −34°C, and Z10 verging towards half-hardy to about −1°C.

AGM: RHS Award of Garden Merit.

GROUP 1: SHORT-LIVED PLANTS

This group includes annuals, biennials, and perennials that rarely live longer than four years without needing replacement. As they are short-lived, some have a propensity to produce a lot of viable seed.

E. biumbellata Z8   Eastern Mediterranean
An upright species, best grown as an annual from seed. A fully-grown plant at around 50cm has stems topped with two umbel-like structures – hence the specific

name – producing a hazy, dull yellow mass of flowers from early summer onwards. Needs full sun and well-drained soil.

E. corallioides (coral spurge) Z7 — Italy/Sicily

This is a short-lived perennial or biennial which, when established, will seed around. The pretty coral-pink upright stems are topped by a branching system of flowering stems from May–July. The flower colour is yellow, and the stem-leaves light green and hairy, dropping off to leave bare stems as the plant ages. Up to 1m.

E. helioscopia (sun spurge) Z6 — Europe/Asia

The sun spurge is a hardy annual originating from Europe and Asia but now found on every continent. It seeds around easily and, depending on where the seed germinates, can reach 30cm, with flowers from lime to yellow.

E. hyberna (Irish spurge) Z6 — Western Europe

This British native has quite large, dark green leaves, and branching inflorescences from April to summer. The main floral colour comes not from the bracts but from the bright yellow nectaries. It has a compact habit and will cope with shade, making it a good choice for the informal garden. 60cm.

E. hypericifolia Diamond Frost = 'Inneuphe' — Garden Origin

Grown as a half-hardy annual and often used as a bedding or container plant. Typically 30–45cm tall, it produces a non-stop profusion of tiny white flowers from late spring to the frosts. A very pretty plant which needs a well-drained soil in full sun to part shade.

E. lathyris (caper spurge, mole plant or molewort) Z7 — Southern Europe

This biennial species is like no other, being very distinct and easy to recognise. The long, pointed, glossy-green leaves have a strong white midrib and it is the only hardy species where the leaves are arranged in opposite pairs and at right angles to the ones above and below. The plant has a single stem at ground level, branching further up, with a much-branched inflorescence towards the top. The flowers appear from May onwards and have large, unusually shaped mid-green floral leaves with yellow nectaries. By the end of the second year, masses of large fruit and seeds are produced, and if these are not dead-headed, many self-sown seedlings will appear the following spring. In a sunny position and fertile soil this plant can grow to 1.5m in its second year, but can be much smaller in less favourable conditions.

E. marginata (snow on the mountain) Z10 — North America

A tall upright species, best treated as a half-hardy annual where late planting out will ensure the plant performs from summer up to October. The floral leaves are unusual in that they have white margins, hence the common name. Needs full sun and a rich soil which doesn't dry out.

E. oblongata Z7   Eastern Mediterranean

A short-lived perennial, up to 60cm, with pinkish stems branching towards the top and yellow flowers, which are produced virtually throughout the year. The plant can become bare and leggy after a year or two and is best replaced. Propagation should not be a problem as there will always be self-sown seedlings around the garden.

E. paralias (sea spurge) Z10   Europe/Middle East

A British native, growing on beaches and sand dunes from East Anglia and Wales to the western and southern coasts of Europe, as far south as Israel. Small, pale blue-grey, evergreen leaves are topped with small yellow flowers from May to August. The sea spurge is not easy to keep going in inland gardens, preferring a sandy soil and winter shelter, so at best will be a short-lived perennial. Up to 60cm.

E. portlandica (Portland spurge) Z8   Western Europe

This is a small, semi-prostrate species, growing up to 15cm. Pink stems support spoon-shaped green-grey leaves and lime-yellow flowers from April–July. The stems and leaves turn bright red in the autumn. A native to British and European coasts, but growing on cliffs and scree slopes rather than beaches. A short-lived perennial but easy to propagate by seed.

E. stricta (syn. E. serrulata) Z6   Europe

A biennial species which will tolerate most soils and aspects. It has pink, upright stems up to 90cm, with small, pointed, light-green leaves. Many tiny yellow flowers are produced from spring to summer in its second year, giving the plant a frothy, foamy appearance. After flowering, the bracts take on an orange tone and look very handsome, but don't admire them for too long, as this species is an enthusiastic seeder.

GROUP 2: SHRUBS

This group all have woody stems, which persist throughout the year. They can be pruned and shaped like any other shrub. Although this can be done at any time of year the best time in general is late winter.

E. acanthothamnos (Greek spiny spurge) Z9   Greece/Turkey

A rounded shrub, growing to 50cm tall and more across. Tiny yellow flowers are produced from March to May. Unusual in that it is deciduous in summer, shedding its leaves after it has flowered and dispersed its seed. This reveals the mass of thorny stems on the thin branches, giving rise to the common name. It needs a sheltered, sunny, free-draining spot.

E. ceratocarpa Z8   Sicily/Southern Italy

An excellent species, with woody stems topped with wiry, pink, new growth and thin, light blue-green, evergreen leaves. In exposed sites it may need staking but don't let this put you off as this is one of the longest-flowering euphorbias available to the gardener, covering itself with a mass of vibrant euphorbia-yellow flowers from March until Christmas, and even longer in milder areas. Perfectly hardy but will respond more to a sunny sheltered spot. Can reach 1.1m before being trimmed back in late winter.

E. dendroides (tree spurge) Z9   Mediterranean

Very common in the Mediterranean region, where it will grow to 2m. Flowers profusely from March to May. In England it needs winter protection and is best grown as a conservatory plant, which can be brought outside for the summer.

E. margalidiana Z8   Southern Europe

A relatively new introduction which is proving to be hardy. Thick, woody stems up to 2m high carry masses of yellow flowers. Flushes of flowers are produced from April to December. This is an excellent garden shrub giving height and impact in all seasons.

E. mellifera AGM (honey spurge) Z9   Canary Islands

This is a handsome shrub with large, glossy, light-green evergreen foliage. Each leaf has an off-white midrib and can have a thin maroon edge. The flowers, which appear from late April to May, have a complex structure of glands, and with colour ranging from pale buff to orangey brown. This slightly dull floral colour is more than compensated for by a delicious honey scent, particularly strong on sunny days. A friable, free-draining soil in a sheltered, sunny spot is preferred, but in practice the plant can cope with more exposed conditions. Prune out any frost damage in early spring and the dead flower-heads in summer. It can grow quite tall, around 1.5m. In sheltered positions, odd seedlings may appear in the garden.

E. x pasteurii Z8   Garden Origin

At Oxford Botanic Garden, *E. mellifera* and *E. stygiana* were grown sufficiently close together for them to hybridise. This plant is named after the Oxford University student, George Pasteur, who studied the DNA of young plants and confirmed that the hybrid is roughly 50% *E. mellifera* and 50% *E. stygiana*. It has hybrid vigour, and produces many thick, branching stems as high as 2.5m and a similar spread at the base, but can be pruned hard back at any time of year to keep it at a more manageable size. When not in flower it resembles a rounded rhododendron bush, with dark green, evergreen leaves up to 30cm long. The flowers, which appear in late May and June, are a good yellow and still smell of honey. Many people regard this as a better garden shrub than either of its parents, given sufficient space.

E. pithyusa (Balearic Islands spurge) Z9   N Africa/S Europe

Many branching stems, some of which will not flower, arise from woody basal stems. The evergreen leaves are small, pointed and glaucous-blue. Tiny mustard-coloured flowers are produced from July to as late as October. It eventually becomes a straggly 60cm plant with bare stems, and needs replacing every few years. It is easily propagated from seed, and is useful in a sheltered scree bed or rockery, with smaller plants growing around the base to screen the bare stems.

E. spinosa Z8   Mediterranean

An unusual shrub in that it is only 30cm tall but lies on the ground and can eventually grow to 1.2m across. Masses of branching, extremely thin stems produce tiny, green, evergreen leaves and even tinier yellow and orange flowers from May to August. Suitable for a pot, sunny scree bed or rockery, it can be cut hard back after flowering if it gets too wide. Not easy to propagate, cuttings being the best option.

E. mellifera flowers in May

E. stygiana Z9   Azores

A thicket-forming shrub related to *E. mellifera* and on the endangered list in the wild. Dark-green evergreen leaves with a white midrib are produced on branching woody stems. The lower leaves, when stressed, will turn pillar-box red. Clusters of pale yellow flowers appear on the ends of the stems from May to June (later than *E. mellifera*). Needs a sheltered sunny spot in the garden to thrive. Although taller in the wild, *E. stygiana* will rarely exceed 90cm in British gardens but can be twice that size in width.

GROUP 3: PERENNIALS

These plants will grow and flower year on year. About half the species are evergreen, the other half die back for the winter. Some species will get woody towards the base and could be classed as sub-shrubs, but for the purposes of this listing they are all herbaceous perennials.

E. altissima Z9   Middle East

Quite a rare species with long, straight, upright annual stems which can grow to 1.5m, but more usually 90cm. The stems, which have a slightly downy texture, carry narrow, pointed, mid-green leaves. Lime-yellow flowers appear from May to July. Needs a rich, well-drained soil in full sun to dappled shade.

E. amygdaloides (wood spurge) Z6   Europe

A British native, which can be found all over Europe growing in open woodland. As such, it requires soil with plenty of humus, and dappled shade, but will cope with less than ideal conditions. Stems can have a pink hue to them and carry dark-green, hairy, evergreen leaves. Lime-green flowers appear from March to June. It is a fairly short-lived, clump-forming perennial, but propagation from seed is easy. Can suffer from mildew, especially the purple-leaved varieties. Variable in height up to 75cm.

A number of new hybrid forms exhibiting *amygdaloides* traits have appeared in garden centres in the last few years. Unfortunately, many are short-lived and are not disease-resistant enough to perform well in the garden. The horticultural trade should really act more responsibly by trialling these plants in outdoor garden conditions before micropropagating them by the million and then inflicting them on unsuspecting members of the public with alluring pictures and descriptions. These plants are not cheap, and if purchased in early spring, when they are plentiful and at their vibrant best, having been raised under cover, they will usually need replacing by the end of the summer. These comments also apply to the many new forms of **x** *martinii* (see entry).

'Efanthia' (*E. amygdaloides* hybrid)
Lower stem-leaves are deep green, the upper leaves being maroon. Yellow flowers appear in spring but the plant will struggle through the summer, suffering from mildew. 50cm tall.

Thalia = 'Innthal'
Pointed green leaves can have a red flush towards their tips. Springtime sees the stems produce tight clusters of vivid lime-yellow flowers at 60cm. A compact variety, but will eventually suffer from mildew.

'Velvet Ruby'
The best of the newer hybrids, with good green and maroon foliage in winter. Foliage colour is maintained into spring, when the delicate branching bracts open yellow, flushed with orange. Definitely different and will only grow to 40cm. Seems to be reasonably resistant to mildew.

'Craigieburn'   Garden Origin
A selected form from Craigieburn Garden in Scotland, with upright stems bearing deep port-coloured leaves. Bright, light-yellow flowers appear in April and May, making a pleasing contrast above the leaves. Needs a reasonable amount of spring sunshine for the leaves to give of their best colour. 50cm.

'Purpurea' (syn. 'Rubra')   Garden Origin
A common garden-centre plant. The evergreen leaves are a pretty purple. Bright lime-yellow flowers are produced from March to May. A well-grown plant is a wonderful sight in late winter and early spring. However it can suffer from mildew, especially in summer after it has flowered. To lessen this effect, grow the plant in more sunshine and a well-drained soil. 60cm.

var. *robbiae* AGM Z6   Turkey
Discovered in a wood outside Istanbul by Mrs Robb who, in 1891, brought some back to England in her hat box, hence the common name, 'Mrs Robb's Bonnet'. It is sufficiently distinct from other *amygdaloides* forms for some to suggest that it should be a separate species. Indeed, unlike *amygdaloides*, var. *robbiae* has a running habit. The evergreen leaves also differ in that they are larger and more rounded, being a deep shiny green with a leathery texture. It varies in height, with the leafy stems growing up to 60cm for most of the year, adding another 20cm at flowering time, which is March to May. The bracts are a lime green, but if grown in more sun they will be more yellow. Despite its running habit, which some dislike, it has an Award of Garden Merit and is a great plant for giving evergreen ground cover in dry shade, where it will survive,

thrive and happily flower. As the plant creeps outwards, the freshest growth is always towards the leading edge, often leaving bare woody patches behind. It is therefore a good idea, depending on the space you want to cover, to dig up the outer parts and replant in a tight clump every 2–3 years.

var. *robbiae* 'Pom Pom'   Garden Origin

A much smaller and compact version of its parent, reaching only 45cm. Introduced by Bob Brown from Cotswold Garden Flowers. The leaves at the top of the non-flowering stems are tightly packed, giving it a pom-pom appearance.

var. *robbiae* 'Redbud'   Garden Origin

Similar to the parent but the upper leaves, stem and developing buds all develop a deep red colouring as the shoots crook over, prior to flowering from February well into spring.

E. baselicis (syn. *E. barrelieri*) Z9   Mediterranean

An evergreen species with smooth, grey-blue leaves on stems which vary in habit from prostrate to upright. This gives the plant a rather ungainly appearance. It needs a free-draining soil and is best in a pot or a warm, sheltered rockery, but even then will benefit from some extra winter protection to get it through the harshest of winters. Yellow flowers appear during June and July and then the fading bracts turn a brilliant pink colour in late summer before dying. 40cm.

Blackbird = 'Nothowlee' Z7   Garden Origin

A sport of **Redwing**, selected at Notcutts Nursery. It has particularly deep purple evergreen leaves, and is a great foliage plant during the winter, especially with frost or melting snow on it. Red stems carry dark mustard-coloured bracts which are unusually orange/brown on the reverse. These are produced from March to June. It is a handsome plant but beware, as it can try to revert (just pinch out any plain green stems), and can suffer from mildew if it gets too much sun and dries out. Height 45cm.

'Blue Haze' Z8   Garden Origin

Bred by English plantsman Robin White, this is an excellent hardy hybrid between *E. seguieriana* subsp. *niciciana* and *E. nicaeensis*. It has a cascading habit, being 45cm in the centre, falling gradually to the prostrate outer stems and reaching >60cm across. Small, powder-blue evergreen leaves are topped with sprays of yellow flowers from June to the onset of harsh winter weather in November or December, making it a very long flowerer. Looks fabulous in a large patio pot or a sunny scree bed.

E. brittingeri (syn. *E. flavicoma*) Z8   Mediterranean Europe

Found from Spain to Hungary, it is a variable species, both in height and spread.

E. 'Blue Haze' in June — flowered continuously until December

Green leaves appear in spring on pink stems, which can turn quite woody towards the end of the year. Lime-yellow flowers appear from June to September. Will grow in any ordinary soil which does not get waterlogged. Height up to 30cm.

E. broteroi (Brotero's spurge) Z10   Iberian Peninsula
Upward-arching stems are clothed with bluish evergreen leaves. Lime-yellow flowers with pretty orange-scarlet nectaries are produced in March and April. Will need some protection to get it through the winter, especially in northern gardens. Needs plenty of sun and a free-draining gritty soil. Height 35cm.

E. capitulata Z8   Balkans
This is the smallest spurge that can be grown outside in the garden. At only 8cm tall, it needs careful placement so that it doesn't get 'lost' amongst other plants. A trough or sink in the sun is ideal. Slowly spreading prostrate stems carry small evergreen leaves and support minute yellow flowers in April and May, turning orange as they age. Best propagated by taking small divisions from a mature clump after it has finished flowering.

E. characias (Mediterranean spurge) Z7   Mediterranean
This is a very distinctive and popular plant in English gardens. It is a clump-forming, evergreen perennial which can be very variable in the wild, both in leaf, nectary colour and size. This has led to the species being split in to two subspecies: *characias* and *wulfenii*. They have variable life spans, and can last anything from 5

to 20 years, with an average plant doing well to remain vibrant for 8–10 years. All forms, coming from hot, dry habitats, relish a sunny, sheltered position in the garden with free-draining friable soil, from gritty sand to rich loam. They all have tap roots, which keep the plant alive during the hot, dry summers of the Mediterranean; therefore they cannot be dug up and moved once established, as severing the tap root will kill the plant.

The inflorescence has a definite cylindrical shape, and consists of many quite short branches carrying fused cyathia leaves and all gathered towards the end of the plant's main stems. In winter, the upright stems will start to bud up, and the tip of each stem will arch over and look like a shepherd's crook. This is perfectly normal, and within a month, the stems will unfurl into their flowering shape. *E. characias* has long flowering periods – of months rather than days and weeks. In milder winters, some forms will start to flower in January, and flowers can still be seen in late June. Eventually, after shedding their seeds, the flowers will start to die, turning brown and crisp. Do not dead head, as the whole of the stem will die back and should be removed by cutting it as near to the ground as possible, where new stems will already be growing. These new stems will give the plant its evergreen foliage in the winter, and then produce flowers in the spring, before themselves dying back. In effect, although these are perennial plants, they flower on a biennial cycle.

The two subspecies, *characias* and *wulfenii*, are clearly distinct in the wild, with subsp. *characias* being generally smaller and with darker nectaries, and subsp. *wulfenii* taller, with paler or yellow nectaries. However, all forms hybridise freely and produce large amounts of viable seed. This has led to a proliferation of named forms coming on to the market and the *Plant Finder* lists around 40 varieties. Most seed-grown *characias* plants will earn their keep in the garden, but any good distinct forms need to be propagated by cuttings, as division is not an option. In the garden, the distinction between the subspecies over the years has become blurred and I feel that it is now time for the taxonomists to consider putting *all* cultivars under the one *characias* epithet. This has happened with *Helleborus orientalis* hybrids which are also very promiscuous and are now called x *hybridus*. We need to keep the two main subspecies separate, as these are clearly distinct in the wild, but for the purposes of this book I am no longer going to differentiate between forms of *characias* and *wulfenii*.

E. characias subsp. *characias*
This is the full name given to the basic species, which is distributed throughout the western Mediterranean. It has mid-green leaves which are quite rounded at the tips, and is typically about 90cm tall. The flowers have dark nectaries ranging from dark brown to dull orange (nectary colour can vary on the *same* plant and will certainly change colour as the flower ages).

E. characias subsp. ***wulfenii*** AGM

This is taller than subsp. *characias*, typically reaching 1.2m, and is found in the eastern Mediterranean. Stem-leaves tend to be a pale blue-green and more pointed at the end. The nectaries are generally lighter, coming mostly in shades of yellow to buff.

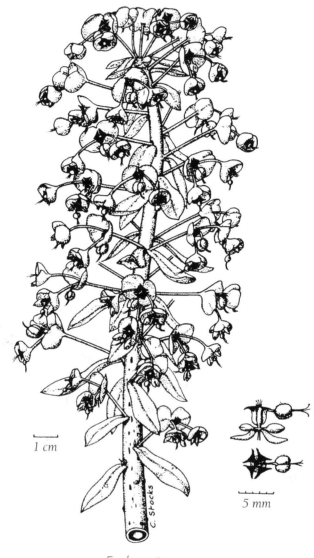

1 cm

5 mm

E. characias

Most named varieties of *characias* are listed here. They are classified into groups according to the main features which the gardener may be looking for, or for identification purposes.

Colourful bracts

'Bosahan'
A selection found in a garden in Cornwall of the same name. A vigorous variety with pale lemon bracts. 1m.

'Goldbrook'
This looks like a smaller form of subsp. *wulfenii*, and has bracts that exhibit a strong yellow colour.

'Lambrook Gold' AGM
Introduced by Margery Fish of East Lambrook Manor in Somerset. It is quite an old variety with golden yellow bracts which still performs well in the garden. The original form often threw up the odd streaked and variegated stem leaf. >1m.

'Lambrook Yellow'
A descendant of 'Lambrook Gold', with very large floral heads and paler yellow bracts. >1m.

'Perry's Winter Blusher'
A selection introduced in 1986 by nurseryman Pat Perry of Whitby. It may produce the odd flower any time from late October onwards. The apical leaves and flower buds exhibit a strong pinkish maroon colour initially, which persists on the backs of the bracts well into the flowering period. 1m.

'Whistleberry Gold' / 'Whistleberry Jade'
These two varieties were originally produced for the mail-order market, and have yellow and green bracts respectively. 'Whistleberry Jade' at 1m is the taller of the two.

Tall varieties

These are the giants of the species, often reaching 2m. They make bold statements in the garden and can either stand alone or be placed at the back of a large border.

'Jayne's Golden Giant'
A vigorous old variety with large golden heads. 1.4m tall.

'Joyce's Giant'

This plant, a seedling of 'Lambrook Gold', appeared in Broadleigh Gardens, Somerset. It can reach 1.5m and has very large floral heads.

E. sibthorpii

The wild form of subsp. *wulfenii* from mainland Greece. It has yellow flowers and can grow as tall as 1.60m.

'Thelma's Giant'

A giant form which Roger Turner had in his garden at Cheltenham. It has greener than average bracts and youthful plants will be 2m tall.

Unusual foliage

These forms have the bonus of unusually coloured or textured foliage, which is very handsome, especially in the winter.

'Blue Wonder'

The more common blue-leaf form with blue-grey stem-leaves. It is not a vigorous form generally, producing only a handful of floral stems and being only 60cm tall.

'Blue Hills'

An old variety and still the best form with strong blue stem-leaves. It produces a lot more flower stems than 'Blue Wonder', and at 90cm is taller. It is, however, becoming harder to track down.

'Portuguese Velvet' AGM

This is a wild Portuguese form collected by John Fielding. The stem-leaves are a rich green and are covered in tiny hairs, giving them a soft, velvety texture. The bracts are quite green with dark brown nectaries. The plant has a slightly open habit and well grown plants will reach 90cm.

'Purple and Gold' (syn. *E. characias* 'Purpurea')

Selected by S. Pawlowski of Yelverton, Devon, this is one of the best *E. characias* forms, with a long period of interest. When the first cold and frosty weather starts in October, the top 30 or more leaves at the end of every stem turn from a typical *wulfenii* green to a lovely purple colour and remain like that right through winter until spring, when they are topped by golden cylindrical flower heads. Eventually the whole stem dies, and new shoots have green leaves until the following autumn. 1.2m tall.

E. characias 'Purple and Gold' in March

'Forescate'

A variety of average height (90cm) and vigour. It has upright stems, the bottom half of which colour up a pretty pink, and the leaves have streaks and splashes of pinky-purple. The cylindrical inflorescences are, unusually, very spaced out.

Coloured Nectaries

These selections exhibit a fairly uniform nectary colour. This colour is at its vibrant strongest in the early stages of flowering.

'Black Pearl'

The nectaries of this form are so dark brown as to appear black, set inside lime green bracts, which makes a very striking picture. Beware of seed-raised forms carrying this name, as they may turn out to be not as black as you want. It is best to buy the plant when it is flowering so that you know what it is like. Up to 90 cm. There is also a dwarf form which is about half as tall.

Dwarf forms

There are a number of dwarf forms available, and they make good garden plants if space is at a premium. However, in *characias* terms 'dwarf' is still not small and they will come in at around 60cm.

'Perry's Tangerine'

Another good introduction by Pat Perry of Whitby. A strong upright plant reaching 1.1m. The nectaries are a consistent dull orange colour, which is unusual and very pretty.

'Starbright'

Thin upright stems to 90cm carry narrow, light-green leaves. The flowers have the palest starry-yellow nectaries.

Variegated Varieties

These make very striking images in the garden and look brilliant with frost on them in winter. But beware, some selections don't like exposure to the winter elements so, depending on where you live, they will need careful placing in the garden, or go for the hardier forms.

'Burrow Silver'

Raised by Mary Benger of Burrow Farm garden near Axminster. It has an upright habit reaching 90cm and has a handsome, broad, pale-cream variegated edge to the leaves. However it does not like cold winter winds, which make the leaves

E. characias 'Perry's Tangerine'

E. characias 'Black Pearl'

turn brown and die, and so needs winter protection even in the southern half of Britain.

'Emmer Green'
A *wulfenii* sport found in a garden in the village of Emmer Green in Berkshire. It will not reach the size of most *wulfenii* varieties, growing to a maximum size of 90cm, and often shorter, at around 60cm. It is a very handsome plant and is probably the hardiest of the variegated forms.

E. characias 'Emmer Green'

'Kestrel'
This appeared as a chance seedling at Kestrel Cottage, Brand Green, Gloucestershire. It has very pale cream leaf margins and grows to around 75cm. A good form, but not easy to find.

Silver Swan = 'Wilcott'
The most popular variegated form at the garden centres. A good, mature specimen makes an eye-catching sight. It can grow to 1m or more, has a wide pale-cream variegation, and the bracts open to reveal dark red nectaries.

'Tasmanian Tiger'

This newest variegated form was originally a selection made in Tasmania and made its way over here from America. It may be slow to establish in the garden but when it does, it will be 90cm tall. It has a good green/cream contrast to the foliage. The bracts, which occur from March to May, are almost all of the palest cream/white, with just small splashes of green. The nectaries are orange.

Variegata

This is the name given to any seed-raised *characias* plants with variegated foliage. Many will have originated from 'Lambrook Gold'. They will generally make good garden plants, but can be short-lived and can be variable in size and leaf variegation. 60cm–1m tall.

Vigorous Varieties

These varieties have been selected for their vigorous production of many strong leafy stems and/or large heads of flowers.

'Humpty Dumpty'

One of the best cultivars, this makes a stunning sight in the garden, but it is *not* a small plant, as it will grow to 90cm. Introduced by Pat Perry of Whitby, this plant has a vigorous urge to produce floral stems, even when small and newly-planted. The original plant produced over 100 stems, and >80 flowering stems are not unusual, giving the plant a tight, dumpy habit, hence the name. The bracts are apple-green, with light brown and yellow eyes. A deservedly popular variety.

'Jimmy Platt'

Named after Jimmy Platt who was assistant editor of the RHS publication, *The Garden*. Another strong-growing cultivar which can grow to 1.2m and is very floriferous.

'John Tomlinson' AGM (syn. Kew form)

Introduced from seed collected in the former Yugoslavia. This is an excellent form, being of a good size, >1m, and producing enormous inflorescences. These are often wider in the middle than at either end, giving a distinct globular or spherical appearance. Ideally propagated from cuttings, but seedlings are often as good as the parent.

Margery Fish Group

This name covers plants raised from seed collected from 'Lambrook Gold'. As such they will be variable but should all make good strong garden plants.

'Spring Splendour'

This is an old form. It makes a large, leafy plant with large, pale-yellow inflorescences throughout the spring. 1.2m tall.

E. cognata Z7   Western Himalaya

A delicate, erect species from Pakistan and Afghanistan. It has mid-green deciduous leaves with white midribs. The stems can develop a light-pink colour and are topped with bright-yellow flowers from June to September. Prefers a rich well-drained soil in full sun and grows up to 70cm.

'Copton Ash' Z9   Garden Origin

A form of *seguieriana* introduced by Tim Ingram of Kent. It has an open habit with small, pale-blue evergreen leaves. Yellow flowers are produced up to 45cm from June to August. This variety does not like winter wet and is only suitable for a dry garden, or grown in a pot and brought under cover for the winter.

E. cornigera AGM Z7   Pakistan/ N India

This is a popular and easily obtained summer-flowering species, growing up to 1m tall. It has a multibranched inflorescence, giving a frothy yellow appearance on top of dark-red stems in June and July. Green annual leaves have a slight maroon edge to them. Due to a mix-up with the naming of imported seed several years ago, plants labelled *E. wallichii* which grow taller than 60cm will probably be *E. cornigera*.

'Goldener Turm'   Garden Origin

A selected form differing from the species in that the strong stems are not as red and the flowers are tighter, with larger bracts having a strong yellow colour.

E. cyparissias (Cypress spurge) Z5   Europe–Central Asia

First impressions are that this is a dainty, deciduous euphorbia, around 30cm tall with a mass of small, thin, green leaves topped by many lime-yellow flowers. It can be seen growing all over the Alps but it is not a typical alpine plant and should *not* be planted in a rockery. In fact, it spreads by underground runners and, if wrongly sited, can be a nuisance. However, the plant can be kept within bounds by digging out any stray growth every spring, as it is not deep-rooted. This is also the best way of propagating it. The flowers, which make an appearance in April, lasting until June, have a sweet perfume which can only be detected at ground level unless the plant is grown in a raised bed or wall. This species and its forms will also repeat-flower in September, which is unusual in euphorbias, as many have such a long flowering period that one flush is all they produce. It can be grown in any soil that receives some sun and doesn't get waterlogged, but will run more on light soils.

E. characias 'John Tomlinson'

Suitable for pots, confined areas like dry-stone walls, or as ground cover amongst tough shrubs.

'Bushman Boy'   Garden Origin
First called 'Bush Boy' and introduced by Gary Dunlop of Ballyrogan Garden in Northern Ireland. It is smaller than the species at 20cm and is a much-branched form, giving it a feathery appearance.

'Clarice Howard' (syn. *cyparissias* 'Fens Ruby')   Garden Origin
Found in a West Yorkshire garden by Howard Bateman, this variety is generally taller than the species' at 40cm. The new growth emerging in late winter has deep-red/maroon leaves. These are later topped by small sprays of yellow flowers from April to June, making a particularly attractive combination.

'Fens Ruby' (syn. *cyparissias* 'Clarice Howard' and 'Purpurea')   Garden Origin
Of average height at 30cm. The emerging leaves are more purple than 'Clarice Howard', becoming lighter with age. Yellow flowers appear from April to June and again in September. Plants in the trade under the name 'Red Devil' are indistinguishable from 'Fens Ruby'.

E. cyparissias 'Clarice Howard'

'Orange Man' Garden Origin

The yellow floral leaves have a definite orange tint to them which eventually fades as the flower ages. Then as late autumn arrives, the green stem-leaves will have orange shades as they die back for winter. It is very vigorous and regarded by some as a thug. 40cm.

'Tall Boy' Garden Origin

Another introduction by Gary Dunlop, at 50cm it is the tallest cultivar. Long, straight, green stems are clothed with much larger leaves than average. The stems are topped with well-spaced yellow flowers over the same period as the species.

E. donii Z7 Himalaya

Often seen in nurseries under the name of *E. longifolia*, but this is an invalid name. A handsome, deciduous species with strong, straight stems which mature to a height of 1.2m. The relatively long leaves have a strongly marked maroon edge all the way round and a distinct midrib. Bright yellow flowers are produced over a long period of time, starting in June and lasting all summer.

'Amjillasa'
A more compact (up to 90cm) and upright form, introduced via seed collected in Pakistan near the village after which it is named.

E. dulcis Z4   Europe
An unusual and easily distinguishable species as it has thick rhizomes, usually visible at ground level. The annual stems make a neat dome up to 50cm but often less. The stem-leaves are rounded and plain mid-green, as are the bracts; the only other floral colour being the tiny red nectaries. The flowering period is April and May. In late summer and early autumn the stem-leaves will turn pretty shades of red, orange and yellow before falling. It is best grown in a moisture-retentive soil in sun or part shade. In dryer soils it may become mildewed and defoliated in summer. A clump-forming perennial which could seed around.

'Chameleon'   Garden Origin
Ten years ago this was an extremely popular plant, and justifiably so, as it made a handsome mound, up to 75cm, of small maroon leaves and bracts throughout the spring. Also, seedlings as good as the parent plant would appear around the garden, so it was easily passed around and sold at plant sales. However, it suffers badly from mildew, and also rust in a wet spring, and the plants are weakened. Good specimens can still be found in gardens but they are much less common and tend not to seed as they used to.

E. esula Z7   Europe
This has a large number of untidy annual stems growing up to 80cm. Lime-yellow flowers appear in May and June. It is a vigorous spreader and one that most gardeners will want to avoid.

Excalibur = 'Froeup' AGM Z7   Garden Origin
This chance seedling was spotted at Fromefield Nursery near Romsey, Hampshire. It is probably a hybrid between *E schillingii* and *E cornigera*. These are both summer-flowering species and accordingly **Excalibur** produces branching yellow flowers from late May to August on stems 90cm tall. Most notable are the new stem-leaves emerging in late winter and early spring. These exhibit gorgeous colours, being marbled green with wide, deep, maroon edges, and the midribs and outer leaves are flushed with bright pink. They are a wonderful sight in late winter. By the time of flowering, only the maroon edge remains. Propagate by cuttings or by dividing mature plants in early spring.

44

E. fragifera (strawberry spurge) Z6   Balkans

A handsome, but rare species, related to *E. polychroma* and, from a distance, looking very similar. All cultivation requirements are the same as for *E. polychroma*. It is a deciduous species which grows into a neat mound 45cm tall. The chrome-yellow flowers are large and well spaced out, appearing in May and June, slightly later than *E. polychroma*. The bracts develop orange-red tints with age, as do the seed pods, which look superficially like strawberries, hence the common and specific names.

E. glauca (Maori spurge) Z9   New Zealand

This is a unique species in more ways than one. First, it has evolved in New Zealand, thousands of miles away from anything remotely similar. Second, there are no floral leaves. All stem leaves are a pale, glaucous blue and the cyathia and nectaries are a deep red, giving the plant a most unusual appearance. The bractless flowers appear from June to August. It is evergreen, grows up to 60cm, and has a slight tendency to run, but not enough to be a problem. It needs a rich, free-draining soil and plenty of sun; in many parts of the UK it will be short-lived without some winter protection.

E. griffithii (Griffith's spurge) Z5   Himalaya

Unmistakable, as the only hardy species to have bright red-orange bracts. It is also the only Himalayan species that flowers as early as May, which is its peak flowering month. Often found in moist habitats in the eastern Himalaya, it prefers a good moisture-retentive soil in a reasonably sunny spot. The thick, underground roots may travel up to a metre in different directions, and large spreading clumps are not uncommon, especially if the soil is light and dry. This trait does not endear it to some gardeners. However some of the forms are not as rampant as the species and there is no doubt that, en masse, the plants make a stunning contribution to the garden border in spring. Annual stems start their growth in early March, which is the best time to propagate from divisions or to dig out unwanted growth if space is limited. Handsome pointed green leaves, often with red midribs, clothe the 80cm dark red stems before the flowers appear. Stems can be cut down to ground-level in autumn as they die, but may need to be cut down earlier if they defoliate in late summer.

'Dixter' AGM   Garden Origin

An excellent form selected by Christopher Lloyd of Great Dixter Garden from seedlings grown by Hilda Davenport-Jones of Washfield Nursery, Kent. The most noticeable difference from the species is that the stem-leaves are much darker, being a deep bloodshot colour with a pinkish-grey colour beneath. It has vermilion-red flowers in April and May. Not as vigorous as the species and usually described as growing to 60cm, but will grow taller and may reach 90cm.

E. fragifera in May

E. glauca in July, with bractless flowers

'Dixter Flame' — Garden Origin

A selected form of 'Dixter' introduced by Gary Dunlop of Northern Ireland. It is taller than Dixter at >1m, and the flowers are more of a flame orange.

'Fern Cottage' — Garden Origin

A variety selected by Clive Jones of Cumbria and named after his house. The stem-leaves are a darker green and the flowers are pale orange. There is no discernible difference between this variety and the variety 'Wickstead'. 90cm tall.

'Fireglow' — Garden Origin

This is the most popular of the *griffithii* cultivars and is a common sight in British gardens in the spring. It was originally introduced by Alan Bloom of Bressingham and has bright red flowers with yellow nectaries from April to June. The stem-leaves are clear green. This is a first-rate garden perennial and in the right conditions can grow to 1.2m. Over the years, seed-raised forms have appeared on the market with an inevitable variation in the floral colour; some forms are not as fiery as the original clone, so it is best to see the plant in flower before purchasing.

E. griffithii 'Fireglow' in May

'King's Caple'   Garden Origin

A fine variety introduced by Mrs Taylor of King's Caple, Ross-on-Wye. It is a
bushy, free-flowering form, reaching 1m in height. The large floral heads are a
subtle orange colour and are held well above the foliage. They make a very
pretty sight in direct sun or when illuminated by sunlight from behind.

E. jacquemontii Z7   Himalaya

From Pakistan to Tibet, this is a smaller and more delicate looking species than
others from the Himalaya. The thin, green, annual leaves are very attractive, with
wide maroon margins and thick white midribs, giving a striped tricolour
appearance. The dull-yellow flowers appear from May to July. Reaching only 50cm,
this species is suitable for the front of a summer-flowering border.

'Jade Dragon' Z7   Garden Origin

A garden hybrid with some *characias* and *amygdaloides* characteristics. The green
leaves are hairy and quite lax. The whole plant at 60cm has a drooping, untidy habit
and the flowers have jade-green bracts in spring.

'Jessie' Z7   Garden Origin

A tall (>1m), interspecific hybrid between *EE. griffithii* and *polychroma*, from
Sunfarm Nursery in the USA. It flowers in spring and exhibits characteristics of
both its parents, having vivid yellow bracts with orange/red rims. This colouring
melts into the top stem-leaves. The plant is sterile and sets no seeds.

E. x *martinii* AGM Z7   France

A natural hybrid between *E. characias* and *E. amygdaloides* found in a ditch in
central France. Deep-red stems support green, evergreen leaves with a hint of
purple, which becomes stronger through the winter. Cylindrical inflorescences
appear from March to July, with individual flowers having a pale green bract and
distinct red eyes. Repeat flowering may occur in October. Will grow in ordinary soil
in sun to part shade. Plants can be variable, growing up to 75cm, and may suffer
from mildew, shortening the plant's life.

'Helen Robinson'   Garden Origin

Originating in the RHS Hyde Hall Garden in Essex and named after its late
owner. This is proving to be the best x *martinii* cultivar. At 90cm, it is a tall and
bushy plant. The dark green, evergreen leaves look midway between x *martinii*
and *E. amygdaloides* var. *robbiae* in leaf, and the floral nectaries are a lighter
orange/red.

Dwarf forms

An increasing number of smaller x *martinii* forms are available to the gardener.

All have the distinctive red eyes, but some are better than others. If you choose one, enjoy it while it is fresh and vibrant, but don't expect it to last long in the garden, as mildew may well become a problem and the plants may wither and die.

'Aperitif'
The smallest form at 25cm.

'Baby Charm'
Very compact, with tightly-packed stems. Height 45cm.

Helena's Blush = 'Inneuphhel'
The pictures on the plant labels look fantastic, showing pale-green leaves with good yellow margins, and the top leaves heavily flushed with pink. The bracts are also variegated in gold and green. Unfortunately the plant is unstable, reverting to plain green, and is not resistant to mildew. Height 40cm.

'Kolibri'
Bred for containers. Height 30cm.

'Tiny Tim'
Sulphur-yellow bracts. Height 30cm.

'Walberton's Rudolf'
Attractive red-tipped winter shoots precede the flowers. Height 50cm.

E. myrsinites AGM Z6   Mediterranean
A prostrate evergreen species, rarely exceeding 30cm in height, but can reach 1.2m across. Thick stems carry round-edged, but pointed, waxed, blue-grey leaves. Lime-green flowers turn more yellow with age and appear in March and April. The plant needs full sun and free-draining, gritty soil. Also the outer prostrate stems will rot if in contact with damp soil for any length of time, so it is best grown in an alpine sink, raised wall or scree bed with a gravel mulch between the plant and the soil. Propagates easily from seed.

E. nereidum Z8   Morocco
One of the few leafy perennials coming from Africa that can be grown outside in our gardens – just! Needing a sheltered spot in the garden, it will cope with temperatures down to –5°C. If these temperatures persist, then the above-ground growth of this evergreen will become deciduous and die down. Protection of the crown with horticultural fleece will help in this situation. Plants of this species can

E. myrsinites

grow to around 2.3m, with thick stems carrying large, branching inflorescences of yellow flowers, high up. It will flower from July to early winter, when sharp frosts will curtail the floral display. This is a rare species, which makes an eye-catching impact at the back of the border during summer and autumn.

E. nicaeensis (Nice spurge) Z7   Balkans/Mediterranean

Although the name implies that it comes from around Nice in the south of France, it is in fact very variable, with nine subspecies ranging in distribution from north-western Africa to the Caucasus. Described below are the forms that are available to the gardener. They have bluish-green evergreen foliage and require well-drained soil and a sunny aspect. Propagation is difficult, as our summers are often not hot enough to produce viable seed. Division is not an option and cuttings are slow to take.

subsp. *nicaeensis*   Southern Europe

This is the most common form found in British gardens. It has pale pink upright stems with quite large blue-grey leaves, contrasting well with the lime-yellow flowers from late May to August. Variable in height, up to 90cm, but more often 60cm.

subsp. *glareosa*   East/Central Europe

A smaller subspecies, often only 30cm tall, with a more open habit and a slight tendency to run. Khaki-yellow flowers appear from June to August.

'Abbey Dore'   Garden Origin

Although often listed as just 'Abbey Dore' it is obviously a *nicaeensis* form. It originated as a seedling in Abbey Dore Court garden near Hereford. It is an excellent form, with strong, upright, arching stems to 50cm. Large, mustard-coloured flowers top the plant from July to September.

E. palustris (swamp spurge) AGM Z6   Eastern Europe to China

A large clump-forming perennial that has a huge habitat range across Asia. It prefers moist soil but will cope with most soils in sun or part shade. The annual stems grow to around 1m before the yellow flowers appear from April to June. After flowering, side-shoots continue to grow during the summer and can reach 1.5m, which may necessitate staking to stop it encroaching on adjacent plants. The leaves are green in spring and summer, turning to pale yellow and even red before they drop in autumn.

'Walenburg's Glorie'   Garden Origin

A selected form introduced by Michael Wickenden of Cally Gardens, Scotland. A clump-forming perennial very similar to, but more refined than the species. It does not make quite such a large plant. 1.2m.

E. x *paradoxa* Z7   Eastern Europe

A natural hybrid between *EE. esula* and *salicifolia*. This is a vigorous runner which most gardeners will want to avoid.

E. pekinensis Z5   Eastern Asia

Hairy grey-green annual leaves appear in spring on bright pink stems. Pale yellow flower-heads are produced in June and July at up to 60cm. In autumn the plant turns a fiery red before dying back. Needs rich soil with more sun than shade. This is a very colourful but rare species and is not easy to find.

E. polychroma (cushion spurge) AGM Z5 (syn. *E. epithymoides*)
Central Europe

Linnaeus originally named this species *E. epithymoides*. However, most gardeners and the horticultural trade now use *E. polychroma*, as does the RHS *Plant Finder*. The specific name means 'many colours', and although the floral colour is constant, the leaves and stems add a variety of colours. All forms make excellent spring-garden perennials with a long list of virtues: they are very hardy; seed around very little and don't run; they make a neat, compact mound (hence the common name) which never needs staking. The most stunning floral displays will be produced when plants are grown in full spring sunshine, but they will produce a fine show in more shady conditions. All the varieties are easy to grow and will tolerate a wide range of garden soils. Mature plants can be divided in late winter using a sharp knife, as the crowns will be quite woody. All forms will root easily from cuttings taken in early summer from underneath the faded inflorescence. The dying top-growth should be removed in autumn, by which time the next year's growth buds will have formed and be visible just above ground level. Unless otherwise stated, all cultivars produce acid-yellow flowers for a good six weeks, between April and early June, depending on where you live in the country. The plant will make a dome 60cm tall and wide.

'Bonfire' Garden Origin

Emerging green leaves soon turn a bright red. The yellow flowers also have red tones. At only 40cm, it is very pretty when grown well, but as with many red-leaved forms, it can suffer from mildew, and defoliate, leaving only the flower-heads on bare stems.

E. polychroma 'Candy'

'Candy' (syn. 'Purpurea') — Garden Origin

This is the purple-leafed form of the species, and is at its best up to, and including, flowering. The bracts colour up a pretty orange-yellow in April and May. However, the foliage can develop mildew after flowering, and may need cutting back. New growth will be mildew-free the following year.

'Compacta' — Garden Origin

Don't let the name fool you. This is a strong grower, and will produce over 200 floral stems in the right conditions. It is no taller than normal, but with so many stems it can grow up to 1m wide. Very eye-catching in full flower, and may produce a second flush in September.

'Emerald Jade' — Garden Origin

A relatively old variety from Gary Dunlop in N. Ireland. At 45cm, it is smaller than average, with smaller stems and leaves. It may give a second flush in September.

'First Blush' — Garden Origin

This is a petite, variegated form, growing no taller than 30cm. The early spring growth is covered in a strong, blushing-pink colour. The bracts differ from 'Lacy' in that they are more open and have wider cream margins.

'Golden Fusion' — Balkans

From seed collected in the former Yugoslavia, and introduced by John Massey of Ashwood Nurseries. It is robust, with dark green leaves and a long flowering period.

'Lacy' (syn. 'Variegata') — Garden Origin

The original variegated variety, growing to 45cm. Young growth emerging in late winter has green leaves edged in pale cream, with a strong pink hue throughout. As the plant grows, the pink colour gradually fades, and is hardly noticeable by flowering time. The flowers are grouped in tightly packed yellow sprays, giving a very frothy appearance. Grow in full sun for maximum leaf colour, but even then, odd stems can revert to plain green. Watch for these and nip them out.

'Major' AGM (syn. *E. pilosa* 'Major') — Garden Origin

This variety makes the usual stunning display in spring, but differs from the species in that after flowering it will continue to grow throughout the summer and early autumn, making a large dome of mid-green foliage up to 90cm tall. In autumn, some leaves will turn crimson before dropping. This variety is much more popular in the south of England than the north.

'Midas' Garden Origin

This is a superb cultivar, which originated many years ago at The Plantsman Nursery run by Jim Archibald and Eric Smith. It has strong, sturdy stems, which never flop, even after heavy showers. Some of the long leaves have a hint of

E. polychroma 'Golden Fusion', showing slightly earlier flowering on the southern (right) side than on the northern side

purple early in the season and can colour up red in the autumn. The intense yellow bracts are longer than the type, and in full flower, completely cover all the green stem-leaves, turning the whole plant into a brilliant, eye-catching yellow dome. Grow it towards the front of a sunny border where it can show off in the spring.

'Orange Flush' Garden Origin

An attractive, but rarely seen cultivar, selected by Jennifer Hewitt of Cleeton St Mary. Its chief claim to fame is, as the name suggests, that the floral leaves have a strong, deep-orange flush, which persists throughout its flowering period. 50cm.

'Senior' Garden Origin

Shorter than average, at 40cm. The leaves have a maroon-pink hue in places and the seed pods colour up to a pretty pink.

'Sonnengold' Garden Origin

Originating in Germany, this form has pale-pink, lax stems, which give the plant an open, floppy habit. The leaves have a pinky-purple tint and are distinctly downy. May give a second flush of flowers in late summer.

E. polychroma 'Midas' in May

E. x pseudovirgata (syn. *E. uralensis*) Z7 Austria

This is an interspecific hybrid between *EE. esula* and *virgata* which arose naturally east of Vienna and has reached most parts of Europe. It has mid-green annual leaves which are narrower than those of either parent, and the small pale-yellow flowers appear from May to August. Like its parents, it has a running habit, and is only suitable for a wild area or in a large meadow planting to add unusual colour, as at Great Dixter.

Redwing = 'Charam' AGM Z7   [for outside Borded]   Garden Origin

An excellent evergreen form, with a long period of garden interest. It is from a cross between EE. x *martinii* and *characias* which occurred in Bernard Tickner's garden at Fullers Mill, Suffolk. It produces many short stems up to 60cm, making a very compact, free-flowering form. Deep-green foliage is heavily flushed with purple from October through to flowering time in early March, making a colourful dome throughout the five darkest months of the year. The dome then becomes completely covered in large, strongly-yellow bracts, which persist to beyond the longest day. It is disease-free, and will grow in any reasonably well-drained soil in full sun to half shade, making this a great garden perennial.

E. rigida (rigid spurge) AGM Z9   Mediterranean

Related to E. *myrsinites*, this is a more upright species, reaching 60cm. The thick succulent-like, upwardly arching stems produce tapering, pointed pale-blue evergreen leaves. It needs a warm, sheltered, south-facing spot to encourage it to reach its flowering potential. Bright yellow flowers are produced early, from February to April. It is suitable for a large rock garden or scree bed. In colder parts of the country it is best grown in a large pot and brought under cover for the winter - it makes a very eye-catching (and large) sight on an alpine bench.

'Sardis'   Turkey

This is a wild form from Turkey, introduced by Chris Brickell. It is more open in habit than the species, reaching only 45cm tall, and more across. One of its main features is that the edges of the steely-blue leaves, and growing tips in winter, have a distinct purple colouring. The golden-yellow flower bracts often colour up red as they die after the plant has produced seed.

E. sarawschanica (Zeravshan spurge) Z6   Central Asia

One of the large, leafy, clump-forming, deciduous Asian species. The annual stems are quite lax and can grow to 1.5m, so may need staking. Spaced-out lime-yellow flowers are produced from May to August. It makes a useful summer perennial at the back of the border.

E. schillingii (Schilling's spurge) AGM Z8   Himalaya

A robust, upright species collected by Tony Schilling in central Nepal. The annual foliage is rich green, being elongated, with rounded edges and a white midrib. Vividly yellow flowers are produced on top of 1m stems in July and August. This is justifiably a popular choice for the summer herbaceous border.

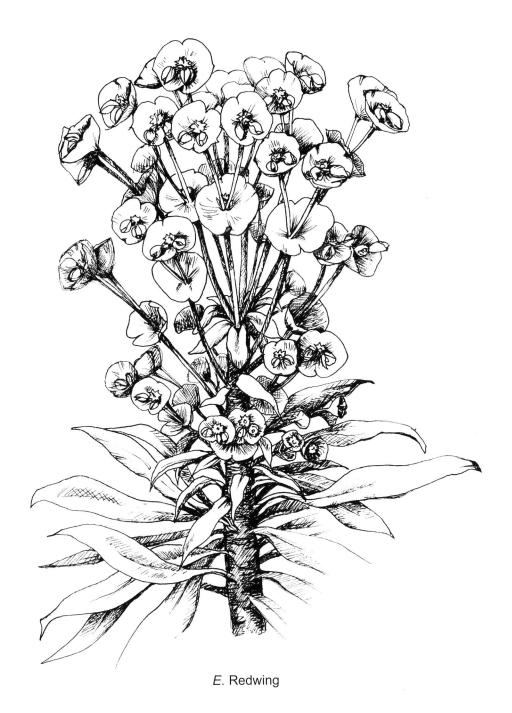

E. Redwing

Association of *Allium hollandicum* 'Purple Sensation' and *E. virgata*, in June

Association of *Ajuga reptans* 'Atropurpurea' and *E. cyparissias*

E. cyparissias clothing a difficult bank under a tree between stream and path at RHS Harlow Carr

E. amygdaloides var. *robbiae* in a shady, inhospitable corner under a tree at Barnsdale Gardens, Rutland

E. seguieriana (Seguier's spurge) Z9   Central Europe-Pakistan

This is an evergreen species with many small, narrow, pointed, lightly glaucous leaves. The stems, which develop from a noticeable woody base in all directions, can grow to 60cm, giving the plant an open, spaced-out dome appearance. Small yellow flowers appear from June to September. It is not a robust species, and will need some winter protection in colder parts of the UK. Suitable for warm, sunny, scree beds or grown in a large pot in an alpine house during the winter months and brought outside in spring.

subsp. *niciciana* (syn. *E. reflexa*) Z8   Balkans/Asia Minor

Having such a wide distribution in the wild, Seguier's spurge has a number of subspecies, *niciciana* being the only one available to the gardener. It is similar to the species, but more compact and robust, and will cope with being outside all year if given free-draining soil and a sheltered, south-facing aspect. More tightly packed flowers are produced from June to October and it makes an unusual front-of-the-border perennial. 40cm.

E. sikkimensis (Sikkim spurge) AGM Z7   Himalaya

This is a very distinctive deciduous species from the eastern end of the Himalaya. The emerging stems and new leaves in winter are a very cheerful, bright, cerise-pink. Although fading as the plant grows, the stems and leaf midrib remain pink through to the flowering period from July to September. Rich yellow flowers develop on stems of 1.2m, making this an excellent summer perennial for the middle of the border. This species will spread, but shouldn't be a problem unless it is grown on light dry soil.

E. soongarica (Dzungaria spurge) Z7   Central Asia

Another of the large, leafy, clump-forming, deciduous Asian species. The annual stems are more upright than those of *E. sarawschanica* and can have a light pink colouring. The green leaves have a noticeable serrated edge and can develop pink and fawn shades in the autumn before they drop. Clusters of yellow flowers appear from June to September at the tops of stems reaching 1.5m.

E. veneris Z10   Cyprus

This species is indigenous to Cyprus, where it replaces the closely related *E. myrsinites*. Thin, prostrate stems have pointed, glaucous, evergreen leaves that are smaller than those of *E. myrsinites*. The flowers are dull yellow, with orange-red nectaries and appear very early, from late January (in an Alpine House) to March. Growing to only 20cm, this is an unusual early-season species grown as a half-hardy perennial.

E. villosa Z7   Europe

Visually, there is little difference between this large, clump-forming, spring-flowering species and the closely related *E. palustris*. Most gardeners will not see a need to grow both species in their garden. Botanically, the young seed capsules of *E. villosa* are hairy, whereas those of *E. palustris* are not. Mature plants grow to 1.2m and have many stems with yellow flowers from April to June.

subsp. *valdevillosocarpa* Z7   Balkans

This subspecies is usually obtained as seed from seed companies. It differs from the type in having much more downy foliage and, at 50cm, is considerably shorter.

E. virgata Z7   Europe–Central Asia

This is a vigorous, running species suitable only for a large area or a semi-wild garden where it can wander at will. Nevertheless, it is a very pretty sight in flower, with lime-yellow flowers from May to July. It will reach 1m and has mid-green leaves which are semi-evergreen in winter. Divisions are easy and it will cope with most soils and full sun to plenty of shade.

E. wallichii (Wallich's spurge) Z9   Himalaya

Most plants listed under this name will be incorrectly labelled and will probably be *E. cornigera*. This is because seed originally imported was incorrectly labelled. The main differences are that *E. wallichii* is much shorter, rarely growing more than 60cm, whereas *E. cornigera* easily reaches 90cm. Also *E. wallichii* flowers in May and June, considerably earlier than *E. cornigera*. Wallich's spurge is quite rare in cultivation and not easy to grow. It needs a good moisture-retentive soil in full sun to be happy.

'Whistleberry Garnet' Z7   Garden Origin

This seedling, probably a cross between *EE. amygdaloides* var. *robbiae* and **x** *martinii*, appeared in the garden of Tessa Hobbs, a garden designer. She passed it on to Whistleberry Nursery in Essex who bulked it up and marketed it. The evergreen foliage is a matt green version of *E. amygdaloides* var. *robbiae*, and the inflorescences are similar to **x** *martinii* but are larger, with orange eyes. It is suitable for most garden soils and aspects. It spreads very little and is easily manageable, making it a first-rate garden perennial, growing up to 90cm.

THE EUPHORBIA YEAR

Here is a monthly list of garden tasks to perform to keep your euphorbias in tip-top condition throughout the year. It also shows when you can expect the varieties to flower, though this is only a rough guide, as flowering times can vary depending on garden aspect, type of season and where you live.

MONTH	GARDEN TASKS	EUPHORBIAS IN FLOWER
January	• Carefully knock off any freshly fallen snow from evergreen species. • Check rooted cuttings and pots under cover, removing any rotting or fallen leaves.	EE. oblongata*, veneris, 'Perry's Winter Blusher'
February	• Plant out new plants in favourable conditions. • Divide and pot up running species late in the month.	E. rigida and 'Sardis', E. veneris, 'Humpty Dumpty', 'Perry's Winter Blusher'
March	• Continue dividing runners. • Plant out new plants and divisions. • Sow seed under glass. • Fork through garden beds and weed.	E. ceratocarpa**, all EE. characias, cyparissias and x martinii forms, EE. hyberna, rigida and 'Sardis', amygdaloides var. robbiae, E. myrsinites, Redwing, Blackbird

Month	Tasks	Species
April	• Beds will benefit from an application of general fertiliser and a mulch. • Prick out seedlings sown in autumn. • Pot up rooted cuttings that have over-wintered under glass.	All *EE. amygdaloides, characias, cyparissias, dulcis* and 'Chameleon', *EE. hyberna,* x *martinii* forms, *margalidiana,**** **Blackbird**, **Redwing**, 'Whistleberry Garnet'
May	• Early in the month, erect stakes around large, leafy forms e.g. *EE. palustris, sarawschanica, soongarica.* • Prick out seedlings sown in March. • Sow seed outdoors. • Late in the month, begin taking cuttings from named *E. characias* cultivars. • Take time to enjoy the spectacular sight of spring euphorbias at their peak.	As above, plus *EE. capitulata, corallioides, griffithii* and cultivars, *EE. lathyris, mellifera, palustris, polychroma* and cultivars, *EE.* x *pasteurii, stygiana, villosa.* Mediterranean forms e.g. *E. niccaeensis* and subspecies, **Redwing**, 'Whistleberry Garnet'
June	• Collect seed from early-flowering forms e.g. *EE. rigida, myrsinites* and *characias.* • Keep weeds down by running a hoe through garden beds. • Keep a look out for any mildew and spray if it becomes a problem. • Water newly planted plants if the weather is hot and dry	Most of the above, plus *EE. altissima, brittingeri, donii, esula, fragifera, jacquemontii, nicaeensis* and forms, *paralias, portlandica, spinosa, stricta, virgata,* 'Copton Ash', 'Blue Haze', **Diamond Frost**, *E.* x *pseudovirgata*

Month	Tasks	
July	<ul><li>Continue collecting seed.</li><li>July and August are the best months for taking stem-cuttings from non-flowering shoots which will have developed from underneath the faded spring flowers.</li><li>Prune out dying flower-stems of spring-flowering evergreen forms to encourage production of new growth.</li><li>Keep container plants watered.</li><li>Pot up strong young plantlets from your spring sowings.</li></ul>	'Blue Haze', *EE. marginata, nereidum, pithyusa, seguieriana, spinosa, stricta*. All yellow-flowering Himalayan species and forms, e.g. *E. cornigera*, and deciduous Asian species, e.g. *E. soongarica*, Diamond Frost
August	<ul><li>Continue to weed as necessary.</li><li>Trim and cut back any large, untidy growth which may be intruding on surrounding plants.</li><li>Pot on rooted cuttings taken early in the season.</li></ul>	'Blue Haze', **Diamond Frost**, *EE. ceratocarpa, margalidiana, marginata, nereidum, pithyusa, sarawschanica, schillingii, seguieriana* and subsp. *niciciana, silkkimensis, soongarica, spinosa*
September	<ul><li>Collect seed from late-summer-flowering species.</li><li>Keep an eye on trays of cuttings and remove any rotting stems or foliage. Water sparingly.</li><li>Dead-head and dig up annual and biennial species (e.g *EE. stricta* and *lathyris*).</li></ul>	'Blue Haze', *EE. ceratocarpa, margalidiana, nereidum, seguieriana* and subsp. *niciciana, silkkimensis, pithyusa*, plus a second flush of *E. cyparissias* and cultivars

October	• Complete harvesting late-ripening seed. • Remove all stakes and cut down all deciduous species to ground level. • Prepare garden beds for planting up by thorough digging and incorporating humus and/or grit. • This is the best month for moving any plants that are in the wrong place. (<u>Not</u> *E. characias* and its forms.)	'Blue Haze', *EE. ceratocarpa, margalidiana, nereidum, pithyusa, seguieriana* and subsp. *niciciana*
November	• Finish cutting back all deciduous plants. • Sow freshly harvested seed in pots, and place outside for the winter. • Move potted-up cuttings and all less hardy species in containers under glass for the winter.	'Blue Haze', *EE. ceratocarpa, margalidiana, nereidum* ****
December	• Remove any straggly or damaged evergreen stems. Stake taller varieties to protect from winter gales if they are in an exposed site. • Fleece less-hardy species and greenhouse cuttings in very cold weather. • Enjoy the winter show of colourful evergreen leaves.	'Blue Haze', *EE. ceratocarpa, margalidiana, nereidum* ****

*   *E. oblongata* can produce flowers during most months of the year.

**   Cut *E. ceratocarpa* back in January and it will flower continuously from March to beyond Christmas.

***   *E. margalidiana* will flower from April to December.

**** *E. nereidum* will continue to flower into winter until it encounters severe frosting.

SOME HELPFUL LISTS

Euphorbias can be used in many ways in the garden and, in variety, can be in flower virtually all the year round. With such a large number to choose from, here are some recommendations that may help the gardener to decide which are good choices for their particular requirements. I have given just half a dozen in each list, but many more varieties will also suit. My favourite dozen are listed in order of preference.

EASY AND VARIED AROUND THE GARDEN

All these should be quite easy to source and, if all were selected, they would make a good introduction to the genus.

E. cornigera – summer border
E. griffithii 'Fireglow' – spring border
E. myrsinites – rockery
E. polychroma – spring border
Redwing – winter foliage, long flowering
E. amygdaloides var. *robbiae* – dry shade

WINTER FOLIAGE

These are obviously evergreen, but give a variety of winter foliage colour. The foliage is especially attractive with a covering of frost.

E. characias 'Emmer Green'
E. characias 'Purple and Gold'
E. **x** *pasteurii*
E. rigida 'Sardis'
'Velvet Ruby'
'Whistleberry Garnet'

LONG FLOWERING SEASON

These spend more time in flower than not, and contribute colour to the borders for an incredibly long time.

'Blue Haze' (May-Dec.)
E. ceratocarpa (Mar.-Jan.)
E. margalidiana (Apr.-Dec.)
E. nereidum (June-Oct., later if not frosted)
E. oblongata (most months)
Redwing (Feb.-July)

EARLY-FLOWERING (JANUARY-MARCH)

All these are also evergreen, and by late winter (March) there are many other good varieties to choose from.

E. characias 'Perry's Winter Blusher'
E. characias 'Humpty Dumpty'
E. rigida 'Sardis'
Redwing
E. amygdaloides var. *robbiae* 'Redbud'
E. amygdaloides 'Craigieburn'

SUMMER-FLOWERING (JUNE-AUGUST)

Apart from *E. ceratocarpa* (which comes from Sicily), the best summer-flowering forms come from the Himalayan region.

E. ceratocarpa
E. cornigera
E. donii
Excalibur
E. schillingii
E. sikkimensis

GOOD IN CONTAINERS

All make good choices for pots, sinks or containers and may also be brought under cover for the winter. All are evergreen, apart from E. cyparissias, which looks good in pots and obviously cannot escape and outgrow its space.

E. cyparissias
E. glauca
E. myrsinites
E. rigida
E. seguieriana
E. veneris

TWELVE OF THE BEST

These are my twelve current favourites, but the list could have been longer. Since I compiled my first list, ten years ago, six new varieties have made an appearance, including three that were not in cultivation then. The one constant is that E. polychroma 'Midas' has remained at the top. I love every form of this species, but 'Midas' just has that extra pizzazz.

E. polychroma 'Midas'
E. donii
Redwing
E. characias 'Emmer Green'
E. characias 'Purple and Gold'
E. ceratocarpa
E. griffithii 'Dixter'
'Blue Haze'
E. **x** pasteurii
'Whistleberry Garnet'
E. nicaeensis
E. margalidiana

FURTHER INFORMATION

Information for this book has been gathered from books (see below), personal records, articles in the media, and contacts with horticultural nurserymen and gardeners. But by far the greatest development in the last ten years has been the explosion of information to be found on the internet. Many a happy hour has been spent trawling websites, searching for information or looking for confirmation of some fact or other.

BIBLIOGRAPHY

Brickell, Christopher (Editor) 1996. *The RHS A-Z Encyclopaedia of Garden Plants.* Dorling Kindersley.

Burnie, David 2000. *Wild Flowers of the Mediterranean.* Dorling Kindersley.

Gledhill, D. 1996. *The Names of Plants.* Cambridge University Press.

Grey-Wilson, Christopher & Blamey, Marjorie. 1979. *Alpine Flowers of Britain and Europe.* Collins Field Guide.

Lord, Tony (Editor) 2010. *RHS Plant Finder* 2009–2010. Dorling Kindersley.

McIndoe, Andrew & Hobbs, Kevin 2005. *Herbaceous Perennials* (Hillier Gardener's Guides). David & Charles.

Metcalf, Lawrie 2009. *Know Your New Zealand Native Plants.* New Holland Publishers (NZ).

Perez, Miguel A. C. 1999. *Native Flora of the Canary Islands.* Everest Editorial (Spain).

Phillips, Roger & Rix, Martyn 1993, 1994. *Perennials* Vols 1(Early Perennials) & 2 (Late Perennials). Pan Garden Plant.

Phillips, Roger & Rix, Martyn 1994. *Shrubs.* Macmillan.

Rice, Graham (Editor) 2006. *The RHS Encyclopaedia of Perennials.* Dorling Kindersley.

Streeter, David & Garrard, Ian 1998. *The Wild Flowers of the British Isles*. Midsummer Books.

Sterndale-Bennett, Jane 2006. *The Winter Garden* (Hillier Gardener's Guides). David & Charles.

Turner, Roger 1998. *Euphorbias: A Gardener's Guide*. Batsford.

Walker, Timothy 2002. *Euphorbias*. (Wisley Handbooks). Cassell Illustrated.

Witton, Don 2000. *Euphorbias*. The Hardy Plant Society.

NATIONAL PLANT COLLECTIONS OF EUPHORBIA

Mr T. Walker, University of Oxford Botanic Garden, Rose Lane, Oxford, Oxon. OX1 4AZ. Tel: 01865 286690, email: timothy.walker@obg.ox.ac.uk, website: www.botanic-garden.ox.ac.uk. Opening times: Nov–Feb, 9am–4.30pm; Mar, Apr, Sept, Oct, 9am–5pm; May–Aug, 9am–6pm. Closed Good Friday and Christmas Day.

Mr Don Witton, 26, Casson Drive, Harthill, Sheffield, Yorkshire, S26 7WA. Tel: 01909 771366, email: donshardyeuphorbias@btopenworld.com, website: www.euphorbias.co.uk. Opening times: By appt., best time March–June.

MEASUREMENT CONVERSION TABLE

Length/height cm	nearest inch
10	4
20	8
30	12
40	16
50	20
60	24
70	28
80	31
90	35
100 (1m)	39

This series of booklets, produced and published by the Hardy Plant Society, covers some of the most popular garden genera, and some of the more unusual ones. Written by experts in their field, each booklet contains cultivation and propagation advice with a descriptive list of some good garden-worthy varieties, including many lesser-known ones. All contain attractive drawings, and the newer editions also contain coloured photographs. They may be ordered by post from the Hardy Plant Society at Little Orchard, Great Comberton, Nr Pershore, Worcs. WR10 3DP.

Other Booklets in the HPS Series:

- *Astilbe, Bergenia & Rodgersia* in the family *Saxifragaceae*

- Campanulas in the Garden

- Epimediums and other Herbaceous *Berberidaceae*

- Ferns

- Grasses

- Hardy Geraniums for the Garden

- Heucheras

- Hostas

- Irises

- Penstemons

- *Phlox*

- Pulmonarias

- Success with Seeds

- Umbellifers